AMERU

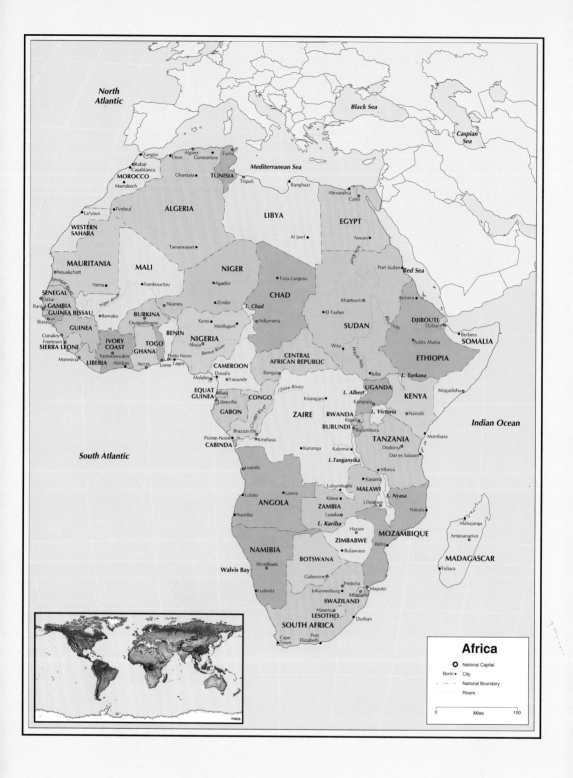

North
Atlantic

Black Sea

Caspian
Sea

Tangier
Rabat
Casablanca
MOROCCO
Marrakech

Algiers
Oran Constantine
Ghardaia

Tunis
TUNISIA

Mediterranean Sea

Tripoli

Banghazi

Alexandria
Cairo

La'youn

WESTERN
SAHARA

ALGERIA

LIBYA

EGYPT

Tindouf

Tamanrasset

Al Jawf

Aswan

MAURITANIA

Nouakchott

MALI

NIGER

Port Sudan   Red Sea

Nema   Tombouctou

Agadez

Faya-Largeau

CHAD

Khartoum

Asmera

SENEGAL
Dakar
Banjul GAMBIA
GUINEA BISSAU
Bissau
GUINEA
Conakry
Freetown
SIERRA LEONE
Monrovia
LIBERIA

Senegal River

Niger River
Bamako

Niamey

Zinder

L. Chad

Ndjamena

Blue Nile

Nile River

El Fasher

SUDAN

DJIBOUTI
Djibouti

Berbera

SOMALIA

BURKINA
Ouagadougou

Kano
Maiduguri

BENIN
NIGERIA
Abuja

IVORY
COAST
Yamoussoukro
GHANA   TOGO
Accra
Lome

Porto Novo
Lagos

Benue River

CAMEROON
Douala
Yaounde

Wau

White Nile

Juba

Banguic

Adis Ababa

ETHIOPIA

L. Turkana

Mogadishu

Abidjan

CENTRAL
AFRICAN REPUBLIC

Malabo
EQUAT
GUINEA   Bata
Libreville

(Zaire River)

Kisangani

L. Albert

UGANDA
Kampala

L. Victoria

KENYA

Nairobi

GABON

Congo River

CONGO

ZAIRE

RWANDA
Kigali
BURUNDI
Bujumbura

Mombasa

Indian Ocean

South Atlantic

Brazzaville
Pointe-Noire
Kinshasa
CABINDA

Kananga

Kalemie

L. Victoria

TANZANIA
Dodoma

Dar es Salaam

L.Tanganyika

Mbeya

Luanda

Lubumbashi

Kasama

Lobito   Luena

MALAWI   L. Nyasa

ANGOLA

Namibe

ZAMBIA
Lusaka
L. Kariba

Kitwe
Lilongwe

Nacala

Mahajanga

Harare

Antananarivo

NAMIBIA

Windhoek

Walvis Bay

BOTSWANA

ZIMBABWE
Bulawayo

MOZAMBIQUE

Beira

MADAGASCAR

Toliara

Gaborone

Pretoria
Johannesburg
Mbabane

Maputo

Luderitz

SWAZILAND
Maseru
LESOTHO

Durban

SOUTH AFRICA

Cape
Town
Port
Elizabeth

Africa

⊛ National Capital

Bonn •   City

—·—   National Boundary

——   Rivers

0   Miles   100

The Heritage Library of African Peoples

AMERU

Esther Wangari, Ph.D.

THE ROSEN PUBLISHING GROUP, INC.
NEW YORK

Published in 1995 by The Rosen Publishing Group, Inc.
29 East 21st Street, New York, NY 10010

First Edition

Manufactured in the United States of America

Library of Congress Cataloging-in-Publication Data

Wangari, Esther.
    Ameru / Esther Wangari. — 1st ed.
       p. cm. — (The heritage library of African peoples)
    Includes bibliographical references and index.
    ISBN 0-8239-1766-5
    1. Meru (African people)—Juvenile literature. I. Title.
II. Series.
DT433.545.M47W36   1995
967.6′24—dc20   94-30208
                                             CIP
                                             AC

Contents

INTRODUCTION

THERE IS EVERY REASON FOR US TO KNOW something about Africa and to understand its past and the way of life of its peoples. Africa is a rich continent that has for centuries provided the world with art, culture, labor, wealth, and natural resources. It has vast mineral deposits, fossil fuels, and commercial crops.

But perhaps most important is the fact that fossil evidence indicates that human beings originated in Africa. The earliest traces of human beings and their tools are almost two million years old. Their descendants have migrated throughout the world. To be human is to be of African descent.

The experiences of the peoples who stayed in Africa are as rich and as diverse as of those who established themselves elsewhere. This series of books describes their environment, their modes of subsistence, their relationships, and their customs and beliefs. The books present the variety of languages, histories, cultures, and religions that are to be found on the African continent. They demonstrate the historical linkages between African peoples and the way contemporary Africa has been affected by European colonial rule.

Africa is large, complex, and diverse. It encompasses an area of more than 11,700,000 square miles. The United States, Europe, and India could fit easily into it. The sheer size is an indication of the continent's great variety in geography, terrain, climate, flora, fauna, peoples, languages, and cultures.

Much of contemporary Africa has been shaped by European colonial rule, industrialization, urbanization, and the demands of a world economic system. For more than seventy years, large regions of Africa were ruled by Great Britain, France, Belgium, Portugal, and Spain. African peoples from various ethnic, linguistic, and cultural backgrounds were brought together to form colonial states.

For decades Africans struggled to gain their independence. It was not until after World War II that the colonial territories became independent African states. Today, almost all of Africa is ruled by Africans. Large numbers of Africans live in modern cities. Rural Africa is also being transformed, and yet its people still engage in many of their age-old customs and beliefs.

Contemporary circumstances and natural events have not always been kind to ordinary Africans. Today, however, new popular social movements and technological innovations pose great promise for future development.

George C. Bond, Director
Institute of African Studies
Columbia University, New York

This woman wears ornaments and skins typical of the Ameru.

chapter

1

THE PEOPLE OF MERU

MANY ETHNIC GROUPS HAVE THEIR OWN STORY of origin. What people believe to be their history can be documented fact or myths. Either way, the story is believed by the people themselves, and it is taught to each new generation of children. The origins of the Ameru are found within the memories of elders of the community. This information is difficult to obtain. Some of the elders who knew the most about Ameru history are now dead. Some elders are reluctant to reveal the secrets of the past. The Ameru did not always have a method of writing. They passed on important information by means of oral tradition.

Some historians argue that the Ameru came from an area around the Niger River in West Africa. They traveled through the Congo Basin up to Kantanga, where they moved toward the

eastern part of Kenya. According to these historians, the Ameru arrived at Mt. Kenya as a
single group with a common language and
culture. They were known as Ngaa. The name
Meru comes from a Maasai word, Mieru, or
Mweru. Some believe this word means, "Those
who cannot speak Maasai." Others believe that
the word means a cold place, perhaps referring
to the icy wind blowing from the top of Mt.
Kenya. The Ameru settled in what is now called
the Meru District.

Meru oral tradition disagrees with this historical account of their origin. The Ameru trace
their ancestry from *Mbwaa*, which is a Swahili
word meaning "island." Thus some historians
believe that the Ameru must have come from a
Swahili area, most likely Mombasa, a city in
southeastern Kenya.

Ameru elders believe that Mbwaa is in Egypt.
According to their oral history, the Ameru were
captured and enslaved by the Nguu-Ntune or
Red Clothes. The Ameru political leader,
Koomenjwe, and spiritual leader, Mugongai,
petitioned for their freedom. The Red Clothes
said that the Ameru could buy their freedom by
performing certain tasks. The Ameru performed
all the tasks except one: making a spear long
enough to reach from the ground to the sky.
This was clearly impossible: The only alternative
was escape.

An Ameru Legend: A Chosen Child

Once a little child lay sleeping in his bed. He was very young, and his second teeth had not yet pushed out his little first teeth. This was the child chosen by the Nkoma, the ancestral spirits, to receive a very special gift.

The Nkoma came in the night to the child's bed. They bundled him up silently and whisked him away to their forest grove, where no living being is welcome without being taken there by the Nkoma themselves. In the grove they took the child to a pond, and he woke with a start when they splashed him with water. The child was frightened, too afraid to speak or cry out. But he listened with his eyes wide as the spirits sang secret songs of the sacred grove. They sang their own songs of circumcision, not like those that the living sing when boys are initiated. Then the spirits circled round the little child and partly circumcised him. That was meant to be a sign that he was chosen.

A leather bag of tobacco leaves was placed before the wondering child, and a gentle spirit sang about how he would become a great diviner during his life. The child was told that if he looked into the tobacco leaves, he would know the answer to any question that a living person could ask him. He would even know some secrets about the future!

With his tobacco gift tucked into his blanket, the child was taken back to his hut, as silently as he had been taken away. In the morning his parents found the signs that the spirits had left, and soon the village knew that a child had received the power of divining the future. All through his life he served as diviner in the village. On days when he was too tired to be bothered with other people's problems, the Nkoma would appear to him in secret. They would sing that song they had sung in the woods so many years ago, about the powers of the tobacco leaves. And the diviner would remember that it was his duty to use his gift to help the living.

▼ YEARS IN THE WILDERNESS ▼

The Ameru took their essential belongings and fled into the wilderness. They wandered for many years until they came to the shores of Iria Itune, the Red Sea. There the Ameru were faced with another impossible task, crossing the sea. Mugongai, the spiritual leader, consulted his oracle. Oracles were usually animal intestines. The shape and markings of the intestines were believed to answer great riddles. This oracle revealed that the answer to crossing the sea lay within *human* intestines.

Three brave men, Gaita, Muthetu, and Kiuna, volunteered to be sacrificed. Only one man was needed. Gaita's intestines directed Koomenjwe, the political leader, to lay his leadership stick on the Red Sea, which would then separate into two parts, clearing the way to the other side.

Crossing the sea in one group was impossible, since the population of the Ameru had grown considerably while living in the wilderness. Koomenjwe divided the Ameru into three groups. When all the groups had crossed, the sea closed up, swallowing up the Mbwaa soldiers who had followed the Ameru.

The Ameru finally came to settle in eastern Kenya, and there they remain, even today.▲

2
THE LAND

KENYA HAS NINE PROVINCES. EACH PROVINCE has several districts, and each district has a local government. The Meru District is located in Eastern Province.

The Meru District lies on the equator around the slopes of Mt. Kenya and the Nyambeni Mountain Range. It covers an area of 3,830 square miles, and with a population of over one million, it is one of the most populated districts in Kenya. The Nyambeni Range and Mt. Kenya are the two dominant features in Meru. Mt. Kenya reaches a peak of 17,641 feet; the Nyambeni Range peaks at 8,200 feet at its southern crest. For a long time, water ran swiftly down these slopes, causing soil erosion which, in turn, created deep gorges down the side of the mountains. These gorges formed boundaries that

socially isolated the Ameru. They were not only separated from other peoples, but also from other groups of Ameru.

Major rivers flowing from the eastern slopes of Mt. Kenya to the Tana River include the

14

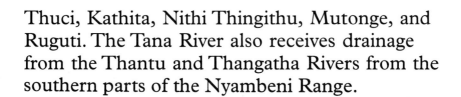

Thuci, Kathita, Nithi Thingithu, Mutonge, and Ruguti. The Tana River also receives drainage from the Thantu and Thangatha Rivers from the southern parts of the Nyambeni Range.

▼ CLIMATE ▼

Short rains fall between March and May; long rains fall between October and December. Rainfall varies within Meru district. The highlands are cooler and wetter than the lowland plains, which vary between arid and semiarid. The annual temperatures vary from 68°F in the high altitudes around Mount Kenya to 91°F in the arid and semiarid lands.

▼ LAND USE ▼

The Ameru have a proud tradition of farming in East Africa. More than 90 percent of the Ameru are farmers. Their population is large, and their land covers both dry and fertile areas. They have learned to adapt to the varying climate and types of soil by growing many kinds of crops, raising livestock, and keeping bees to produce wax and honey. They grow both subsistence crops to feed their own families, and cash crops to sell for money.

In the Upper and Lower Highlands, wheat, pyrethrum, potatoes, maize, beans, tea, and other crops are grown. Livestock, especially cattle, are kept for dairying. Gikuyu, Louisiana,

The Ameru consider this volcano, Meru North, to be sacred.

and Napier grass, clover, maize, and fodder beets are grown to provide feed for livestock.

Many changes were brought to Kenya by British colonialism, which lasted from the 1880s until Kenya won its independence in 1963. These changes included alteration of the relationship between the people and their land. Before the end of the 19th century, most farming peoples grew only the kinds of crops they needed, and only as much as they could eat or store themselves. This changed when the British arrived. The colonial government wanted to make Kenyan land profitable for Britain. The government sold the best land to European settlers, who grew cash crops. Farming peoples were either driven off their land or forced to start growing cash crops.

The introduction of cash crops changed Meru farming systems. The Ameru could not grow enough food for themselves in addition to cash crops for the government. They were also forced to pay taxes for the first time. They had to learn new methods of farming to use their land for the crops the British wanted, or else the soil would be exhausted. The Ameru learned a system called fallowing and shifting cultivation. A piece of land would be divided into several sections. Each section, except one, would have a different crop planted in it. The last plot of land would be left empty, or fallow, to allow it to rest. In the next planting season, each crop would be shifted to a new plot, and a different block of land would lie fallow. Because each kind of crop needs a slightly different combination of nutrients from the soil, this method allows the soil to replace nutrients it has used up, while providing other nutrients.

The land on Mt. Kenya was much different when the Ameru settled there than it is today. Some of the most fertile areas were impassable either because of the icy wind or thick vegetation. Healthy plant life in the Upper and Lower Highlands was protected by a thick bamboo forest that blocked sunlight. For these reasons,

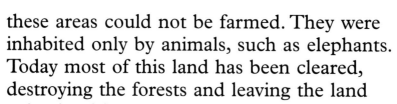

these areas could not be farmed. They were inhabited only by animals, such as elephants. Today most of this land has been cleared, destroying the forests and leaving the land animals without protection.

Below the highlands is the Upper Midland, also known as the Black Forest. Before the land was cleared for modern farming and towns, the region had evergreen and savanna vegetation. Many of the trees were as tall as 150 feet. By the 1890s, the forest had been cleared by the British for beekeeping, livestock-raising, and farming. The major crops grown in this area are vegetables and fruits, including peas, potatoes, carrots, kale, leeks, lettuce, oranges, plums, and bananas.

Crops in the Lower Midland area included sorghum, millet, and cotton. Cultivation was mainly foods such as millet, pigeon peas, peas, yams, cassava, and arrowroots. Sweet potatoes were grown along the steep slopes to prevent soil erosion. Their thick, long roots held the soil in place so it would not be washed down the slopes by rain. Sugarcane and tobacco were also grown. Both of these crops were very important for Meru ceremonies and rituals.▲

chapter

3

MERU SOCIAL STRUCTURE

MANY AFRICAN PEOPLES HAVE A SYSTEM based on clans. A clan is a grouping of people based on common ancestors. According to their oral tradition, the Ameru formed two clans, Njiru and Njeru, when they settled on Mt. Kenya. The two clans are the basis of the Meru social organization to this day.

The two original clans divided into smaller clans. The first five subdivisions were the Igembe, Tigania, Imenti, Miutui, and Igoji. Because of isolation from each other, the clans developed distinct dialects. Although most of the Ameru shared similar beliefs, culture, politics, and economics, the groups developed separate cultural traits. Beyond the first five are further divisions, locations, and subdivisions found in Meru today. These were created either during the British colonial period or after Kenya won its independence.

19

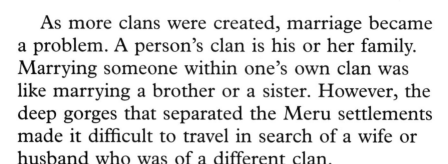

As more clans were created, marriage became a problem. A person's clan is his or her family. Marrying someone within one's own clan was like marrying a brother or a sister. However, the deep gorges that separated the Meru settlements made it difficult to travel in search of a wife or husband who was of a different clan.

It was also taboo to kill a person who was a member of one's own clan. To kill such a person was to provoke the ancestral spirits, who would take revenge on you or your immediate family.

To solve this problem, the elders in each sub-group devised a ritual system known as *gichiaro*, or birth. The ritual formed bonds between people, traced their ancestry, and clarified taboos and acceptable behavior. *Gichiaro* was a belief system developed to help with the social problems of marriage and warfare taboos.

The ritual system was of two types: *gichiaro-mutanochia* (mother-*gichiaro*) and *moanoba* (father-*gichiaro*). If two people were joined by mother-*gichiaro*, they could marry. It was forbidden, however, for a man to kill his mother-*gichiaro* brother.

Neither marriage nor war was allowed within father-*gichiaro*. Such acts were taboo and would anger the ancestors, provoking supernatural punishment that resulted either in bodily harm or madness.▲

chapter

4

CUSTOMS AND RITUALS

As in many African cultures, the Ameru learn their customs through a socialization process that begins at an early age. These customs are part of the whole community's way of life, not just the immediate and extended families. The customs, rituals, and beliefs of the Ameru were inseparable from social, economic, and political structures in daily life. As such, they were guidance for Meru society.

Within the family, the mother plays the major role in caring for the children and the household. Grandparents, aunts, uncles, and children's nurses help the mother. Everyone's role in society is taken very seriously. It is the duty of a community to oversee, give moral support to, and reinforce children in the process of learning their roles. The reinforcement of the codes of behavior was under the leadership of elders, who were the backbone of the society. They were and

Children are held in the highest regard by the Ameru.

still are highly respected and sought after for guidance and oral history. Old age in African societies is associated with wisdom.

▼ ELDERS AND THE LAWS ▼

Before colonialism, the Ameru were governed by a council of elders who were responsible for

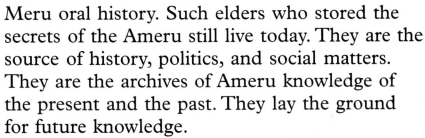

Meru oral history. Such elders who stored the secrets of the Ameru still live today. They are the source of history, politics, and social matters. They are the archives of Ameru knowledge of the present and the past. They lay the ground for future knowledge.

The council of elders was called the *kiama*. Elders from every village were elected by old men and young men who had gone through the ritual of circumcision. The rituals of initiation and circumcision marked the passage of a young man from boyhood to adulthood. Therefore only a circumcised man was thought to be mature and responsible enough to take part in village politics.

The *kiama* was in charge of keeping law and order in the community. The laws were in the form of proverbs, which were memorized and recited as warnings and advice by the elders. The following are some of the most important laws:

1. *Do not laugh at or abuse anyone.* This includes those who are poor or afflicted by deformities. From an early age, a child is taught to think of others with compassion.

2. *Any mother is your mother; respect her.* Children in a community belonged to all mothers to the extent that any mother could feed a hungry child. A mother was seen as a source of nourishment in many African societies. She was like the

Old age is associated with wisdom in African societies like the Ameru.

earth or the soil—the source of resources for
the people. A child was taught to be grateful for
the protection and care of both his real mother
and of the earth, who bore food.

3. *Any elder is your father; respect him.* Whereas
the mother is the source of nourishment, the
father is the source of power and authority
in the community. The Ameru are under a
patriarchal system, meaning that men have con-
trol and power in society. Males are considered
heads of households and breadwinners, although

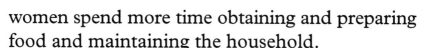

women spend more time obtaining and preparing food and maintaining the household.

4. *Do not steal.* Stealing was forbidden. A thief was sentenced by elders to death. Execution was by covering a thief's head with a skin cloth and dropping him into a river. This custom is not practiced in Meru today. The state has replaced community institutions. Now a thief is put on trial by the state.

5. *Polish your tongue in public.* Communities and public places were important. It was in these places that behavior was judged. How one talked and interacted with others was highly significant.

6. *A circumcised boy shall not eat his mother's food alone.* This taboo was to represent the responsibility an adult male had to his society. "Eating his mother's food alone" is something a child does; a man is expected to think less of his own needs than of those of the community.

7. *The cattle of your father are not bananas to make friendship with.* Cattle are a sign of wealth in Meru society. One is not supposed to boast about one's parents. The idea was that everyone should work hard for his own wealth, not take his parents' herd of cattle for granted. Gaining wealth through livestock involved bravery and military activities. Livestock wealth played various important roles; cattle were used both as food and as a substitute for money.

8. *A circumcised boy should not laugh like a girl.*
The process of gender socialization began at
birth. The custom, based on patriarchal rela-
tions, shaped a man's place in the society. As
head of the household, a man was supposed to
display courage and strength. To behave otherwise was to behave like a woman, and a woman
was associated with weakness. This perception of
women as weak and men as powerful is common
throughout African societies.

Women play major roles in all African societies, including Meru. Women contribute some of
the most basic needs of society, such as raising
children, taking care of households, and doing
production work on the farms. However, men
in these societies generally do not consider
women's contributions as having monetary
value, and therefore they are not appreciated.
Policies for development do not always benefit
women. With women's groups and movements
all over the world, urbanization, and more
education for women, social structures in societies are being challenged.

▼ MARRIAGE ▼

Marriage among the Ameru meant accept-
ance in society. Those not married could not
perform rituals in the society and were seen as
deviants. Parents constantly worried if their
grown children were not married. To get rid of

Women play a major role in Meru society by contributing some of the most basic societal needs, including raising children.

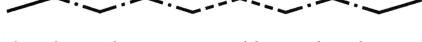

the stigma, the parents would consult a shaman
to find out what should be done for their sons
or daughters in order to marry them off.

The process of marriage was initiated by a
young man. A man searched for an obedient,
beautiful, hard-working, and clean woman.
Gender roles were clearly defined, socialized,
and never questioned. A good wife was, and still
is, one who takes care of children and animals,
cooks, fetches water, collects firewood, works
hard on the farm, has babies (preferably more
boys than girls), and never argues with her
husband.

After a long and thoughtful search, the man
approached a woman for marriage. By mutual
consent, the man visited the woman three times.
Upon the third visit, the mother of the woman
conferred with her daughter about the man's
visit. If the woman was interested in marriage,
the man was officially welcomed in the woman's
home on his fourth visit. Once welcomed, the
man informed his parents about his interest. His
parents then sent a gourd full of honey to the
bride's parents. If the honey was accepted, the
engagement was official. Then the negotiations
could begin for the bridewealth.

▼ BRIDEWEALTH ▼

The bridewealth was a gift, usually of
livestock or other valuable goods, to the bride's

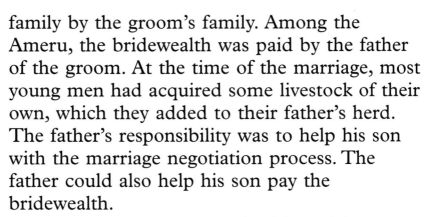

family by the groom's family. Among the Ameru, the bridewealth was paid by the father of the groom. At the time of the marriage, most young men had acquired some livestock of their own, which they added to their father's herd. The father's responsibility was to help his son with the marriage negotiation process. The father could also help his son pay the bridewealth.

Before the negotiation of bridewealth, a gourd of beer was sent to the bride's parents as a gesture of respect. The parents of the bride reciprocated by inviting the father of the groom for a general beer party. Honey was then sent to the bride's family and made into a very strong, sweet wine. A large party was planned. The groom's father, as the guest of honor, was invited to the party together with elders of his lineage.

The next phase involved sending either a bull or a ram to the bride's family. If her family accepted the animal, it was taken as an announcement to the community that they were serious about the engagement. The animal was slaughtered and the lineage of both the bride and groom were invited to the party. Two fifths of the meat was given to the guests; the skin was given to the groom's father.

The actual bridewealth consisted of a cow, a bull, a ram, a ewe, and a gourd of honey symbolizing goodwill and mutual obligations by both parties. The process of give-and-take was never-ending. Finalizing the process of bridewealth was like establishing a friendship between the two families. The process was at times passed on to the the groom's son. Because it was a process of give-and-take, the communities involved did not consider the bridewealth as selling a woman, as the missionaries and colonialists later believed. Instead, the societies of Kenya thought of the bridewealth as a series of gifts and shows of respect from one family to another.

▼ PREGNANCY AND CHILDBIRTH ▼

A newly married couple symbolized new life. They were expected to extend the lineage of their ancestors by having children. The seal of a marriage was pregnancy and childbirth. A marriage that could not produce a child was blamed on the woman. The woman was either divorced or allowed to stay while her husband married a second or several wives. If the second marriage produced no children, then it was the man's fault. The man could do one of two things: divorce his wives so that they could remarry and have children, or ask his brother or a good friend to father his children. In most cases, men chose the latter option.

News of a pregnancy was highly praised not

A Meru marriage must bear children to be considered successful. Children carry the responsibility of extending the lineage of their ancestors.

only by the couple's parents, but also by friends and the community. A pregnant woman was not allowed to perform hard tasks. These tasks were performed by her mother-in-law, in-laws, or the community.

During labor, the woman's mother-in-law and other midwives stayed with her until the child was born. Her husband was not allowed in the house. His duty was to await three cries of

Children are seen as gifts to Meru society. The entire community rejoices in a birth.

joy from a midwife, announcing a successful childbirth. To tell family members the gender of the child, the midwives cut four sugarcanes for a boy and three for a girl. The midwives ate the sugarcane and threw leaves at the roof of the house. To alert the entire community of the child's birth and gender, midwives went out in search of milk for the newborn. The person who gave milk took the responsibility of always having milk available for the child. To tell the community the child's gender, the midwives requested blood from a male cow for a boy, and from a female cow for a girl.

After the cutting of the umbilical cord, the mother was confined to the house until the naming of the baby on the fourth day. If the baby was a boy, it was named after the grandfather; if a girl, after a grandmother. The naming of children alternated between the two parents' families. The first child took a name from the father's family, and the second child from the mother's family. If a female child was followed by a male child, both would be named after the husband's parents. If they were both of the same gender, for example, if both were girls, one would be named after the husband's mother and the other after the wife's mother. The order of naming continued until names of all members of both families were given. After that, children could be named after family mem-

A traditional Meru hut in which a woman may give birth.

bers who had died, or given symbolic names after animals.

▼ EDUCATION ▼

The mother was the foundation of a child's moral behavior. The mother's role was to bring

A child learns proper behavior and morals from his or her mother.

up a child in ways acceptable to the community. It was also the community's responsibility to bring up the child. Education of children went through stages. Different lessons were taught from early infancy through circumcision.

Children were expected to learn their traditional roles in society as they grew. While cooking, mothers or grandmothers would tell stories, riddles, folksongs, and oral history while their children sat at their feet and listened. The children at an early age were introduced to cultural norms, history, and their environment through these traditions. These activities took the place of schools or television. It was the only way to pass on information. Young children occupied their time either playing, listening to stories, or telling stories. Children from seven to twelve years were allowed to go out to play in the evenings. During the day, young boys could join older boys in herding livestock or help their fathers in hunting, beekeeping, and societal duties. Girls joined their mothers on the farms and in household maintenance.

Adolescence was marked by the preparation of the youth to face the world courageously and be responsible men in their communities. Boys stayed in seclusion, going through rigorous training. They were taught moral behavior and how to express their feelings while among women and during courtship. This period ended with circumcision. They then became warriors, defenders of the Meru community until marriage.

Young women were taught to maintain good behavior in general and at the time of courtship in particular; otherwise men would not marry

A Meru circumcisor dressed in clothing appropriate to the significant ceremony.

them. They were expected to learn from their own mothers manners, how to keep their homes clean, how to make their husbands comfortable, and techniques of farming.

▼ THE MILITARY ▼

Young men were involved in military activities. The military had two major objectives: to defend the community against the raids of neighboring groups, such as the Agikuyu and the Maasai, and to acquire livestock as a form of wealth and status. Raids and defense were not confined to outsiders. People who did not belong to the same *ba-gichiaro* were subject to military raids.

The Meru military was under the direction of many leaders. Spears were the main weapons. Warriors had to travel under difficult conditions, camping in the villages of their *ba-gichiaro* brothers. Under the system of *gichiaro*, people who were considered brothers were never allowed to kill each other. Because of this, they were always allies.

Villages served as bases at which the army could rest and acquire food. Women provided the military with food. The method of distribution was woven into the customs and rituals. No woman could refuse to feed those who belonged to her group's *ba-gichiaro* allies. Women were obliged to feed the soldiers millet gruel, milk,

AMERU SONGS OF INITIATION

Iiii baaba ng'ombe, itu
    baaba ng'ombe nyingi

My father has many
    cows; yes, my father
    has many cows.

Ari ma nani ndimukinde,
    aitie ruu akarie
    ndeqwa
Akarie rucii nam
    mutongu. Uuu,
    Kibaru, thira rambu

If I am wrestled down by
    you, I will take you
    home to
eat a bull with us rich
    ones. So watch out!

Kirindi kia Mbugi na
    Murutu
mbitikirieni Kirariri na
    Mkia
na mutue

At this gathering of the
    ancesters of Meru,
sing back to chorus to
    my song
so hard that you almost
    burst.

iii, uuuu, mwiji,
Iru inkware egamba.

Yes, you boy!
It is tomorrow that the
    spur fowl flies
(at dawn, when circumci-
    sion takes place).

Twauma gugaika i
    kerikwa i ja mbui

We have come from a
    boy's circumcision. He
    has paid for manhood
    with pain.

Mwanetu akugura
    kerikwa ja mbui

May it make his life
    straight, as feathers
    straighten an
    arrow.

Young men involved in military activities had two major objectives: to defend the community, and to acquire livestock.

bananas, sweet potatoes, arrowroot, yams, beer, and any other traditional food they requested. Animals, such as goats and sheep, were not given to the army.

The army took only what was necessary for their sustenance while at the village bases. Food was left in empty homes. *Ba-gichiaro* allies would enter and help themselves. After taking what they needed, they would replace the

BLESSINGS

Buragia intu	May your things increase
Mburi, ng'ombe	Goats, cattle
Mwere, uukij	millet, honey
na uria ati na biu	and if someone doesn't have
na we agee	any,
	let him have some.

Eee, ee, ibendwe, ee, ibonthe,	Ee ee, may they be loved by
baciare, bwithe, na bang'ina	all
bagite mburi, ng'ombe	may they have children
baciare aana babaingi muno	may they have goats and cattle
	may they have many many children

CURSES

Antu ibabwe, antu ibabwe	May people be well, may people be well
baithe, bangi'ina, baithe bangi'ina	male female, male female
mburi, ng'ombe	goat, cattle
twiji, twari	boys, girls
baunganie mitwe	may they grow in number
ncai inu ituthame	bad luck, go away from us.
muiji uria uthuraga ungi	The man who hates another,
arora	may he die!
Uria uthuraa antu ba bakwa	Whoever hates my people,
arora	may he die!
muntu uria wagia	The man who does wrong,
nawe arora	may he die, too!
Muntu uria uthuraga ungi	Any man who curses another
akanga: "arora"	and says, "May he die!"
atiramira kuria ruo	he will die right away
rog ut iramira	cursed by people's backsides.

lids of pots upside down as an indication that
the food was not eaten by thieves. Since supernatural beliefs were ingrained in the Meru
system, no thief would dare perform the act of
replacing the lids upside down. To do so would
provoke the anger of supernatural powers who
would punish the thief or his family. Sometimes
army members would dig yams for themselves
from someone's field. However, they could dig
them only on the edge of the farm, leaving the
holes unfilled. Then they would roast them on
a public path. Again, this would show the
farmer that his yams were taken by *ba-gichiaro*
allies.

Any woman who refused to give food to
ba-gichiaro allies, or any ally who did not obey
the rules as stipulated under the *ba-gichiaro* system was punished, but not necessarily by the
community. Spirits of angry ancestors might
take care of it. The punishment manifested itself
in different ways. For instance, if a woman refused to offer gruel, the lid of her gruel gourd
would pop up into the air. If she did not offer
milk, her calves would not suck from their
mother cows. Leprosy and other diseases were
understood as forms of punishment.▲

chapter

5

COLONIALISM

M'AGOCORUA WAS A GREAT MERU PROPHET.
In 1870 he predicted that a strange race of men
would come and defeat his people. Of course,
no one wanted to believe this, but it was an
important part of Meru tradition to take the
prophet's word as truth. Young Meru warriors
debated among themselves. They faced a great
conflict: During initiation, they had been taught
that warfare and success in battle were central
to being a man. But, since childhood, they had
also been taught implicit trust in the prophets
of Meru.

The first European contact with the Meru
was during the 1880s. Here, in fact, was a
strange-looking race, just as M'Agocorua had
predicted. Several decades of debate passed
before it was clear whether the second half of his
prophecy was also true.

A sacred tree where sacrifices were once offered.

In 1906 the Embu, a group neighboring the Ameru, tried to defend themselves against the British colonial government who wanted Embu land for farming. It was a long bloody struggle, and rumors flew to Meru about the plundering, burning, raping, and other inhumane acts of the British. The Embu were defeated, and Meru land was the next target.

Meru elders held many long, intense council sessions about what action to take. Finally they decided that, because of their small numbers and the ruthlessness of the British, it would not be worth losing the lives of most of their warriors to defend the Meru people by force. Some warriors agreed because they felt that they could not possibly defeat this enemy. Other young men strongly disagreed with the elders.

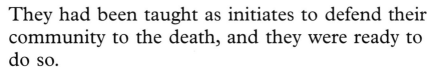

They had been taught as initiates to defend their community to the death, and they were ready to do so.

In the end, the elders had more political power than the warriors. In 1907 they made an extremely difficult decision. They saw that the British could easily kill the entire Meru population because they had much larger forces and better weapons. Therefore, peace offerings were taken to the British commander as a sign that the Meru people would surrender to the colonial troops without a fight.

Although this decision saved the lives of thousands of Ameru, it brought them a great deal of trauma as a people. Meru had one of the proudest warrior traditions in East Africa. No young man was considered a responsible adult until he had staged a successful cattle raid. Physical strength, courage, and independence were central to the Meru image of themselves. Now the Ameru were subjects of the British government. All their customs and rituals were abolished or changed by new leaders forced on them by the colonial government.

The council of elders had been the governing body in each isolated Meru community. Elders were respected for a quality called *ugambe*, or the ability to speak wisely. The British were not interested in the wisdom of old age. Instead they hired younger men to carry out colonial laws

An elder praying.

among Meru society. At this point, the traditional age-set system, where the youngest men were warriors and the oldest were community leaders, was broken down.

At first, in order to pacify the Ameru, the British allowed them to continue certain ritual feasts and ceremonies. However, the colonialists understood nothing about Meru society. The British had outlawed traditional warfare and

Njiru elders decorate their heads before a ceremony.

cattle raids. Most of the Meru feast days cel-
ebrated a ritual called "oathing." This was a ceremony in which young men who were about to
go into battle swore never to return to their
Meru homeland until they had raided a certain
number of cattle or killed a certain number
of the enemy. Although the Ameru were still
allowed to hold the feasts, they were not allowed
to hold oathings or go to war. The ceremonies
thus had no point and soon died out.

One of the most important changes caused by
colonial rule was taxation. The Ameru had never
needed money before. They had used cattle and
gourds of honey as signs of wealth and means of

The Ameru still live a traditional way of life despite their Western attire.

A typical traditional style of dress of the Tigania people, close neighbors of the Ameru. Their traditions are similar to both the Ameru and the Maasai, another local people.

THE RITUAL OF CLEANSING

If a member of *ba-gichiaro* killed another member, only a purification could save him from supernatural wrath. The offender would request cleansing from the elders. The ritual involved presentation of a ram by the offender. The ram was slaughtered by both the family of the murderer and the family of the victim. The ram's blood was sprinkled where the victim had walked. The killer's family would then pay compensation to the family of the man he had killed. The compensation, in the form of livestock, was agreed upon by both sides.

trade. This need for cash was met mainly in two ways: They sold livestock and farm goods, or they labored on work teams for British bosses. Both of these solutions were detrimental to Meru traditions and pride.

Livestock was a sign of wealth. A person could own livestock only if he had won it in a raid. The concept of selling a cow for money

WHAT GOD MEANS TO THE AMERU

Ngai, ne gwe wambombire
na ni gwe umbikerete
    inya
Gantu karia kari konthe
ni ka Ngai
Umbikere inya
unenkere into bionthe
mwere, muya, nthoroko,
    na
mburi na ng'ondu
Umenyere ntikathi
    Kararo
kamwena nkoma

ne untu ukoma imbee ne
    cio
cietaga muntu amami

Ngai, you created me
and you gave me strength
Every little thing
    completely
is of Ngai
Give me strength
give me all things
millet, sorghum, beans,
    and
goats and lambs
Keep me from finding a
resting place with angry
    spirits
because bad spirits are
    the ones
who bring trouble to a
    sleeping man

Murungu, ni gwe wombire
    antu
na ni gwe irungu bionthe

bia mwere, aromba
    kanywa
nyoro, mitho, na
    mugongo

Na ni gwe wombire nyamo
    cionthe
Aromba aromba kinya
    iniore
riti mutiro

Murungu, you created
    men
and you created all the
    parts
of the body. He made the
    mouth
the nose, the eyes, and
    the back.
And you created all
    animals.
He made, he made even
    the monkey
who has no tail.

was foreign to the Meru. Animals were also links to spirits of the ancestors. In ritual sacrifices a certain animal would be chosen for its ability to carry news to the spirit world: A goat was used to symbolize conflict, a sheep for new-found peace. The need to sell livestock left the Ameru without enough animals for ritual, so the traditions could not be passed on.

The warrior age-set suffered the most under the surrender to colonial rule. Not only were they deprived of the opportunity to defend their community in battle, which was their main purpose in life, but they were also forced to work for the British by the need for money. The colonial government had many land projects under way, including the building of roads and railways. The once fierce Meru warriors had no choice but to labor for low wages to pay taxes to their oppressors.▲

chapter

6

A VIEW OF THE FUTURE

THE ENTIRE SOCIAL, ECONOMIC, AND POLITICAL
structure of the Ameru has changed because of
British colonialism and, after a long struggle,
Kenyan independence. The Ameru today can be
viewed only within the context of the Kenyan
state. Because of the land appropriation by
the colonial government, many Meru clan
members were rendered landless. Some of the
landless migrated to nearby cities to earn money
in order to pay the hut and pole taxes introduced by the colonial government. Others
became squatters on what used to be their own
land. Through this process, the family, communities, and division of labor among the Ameru
changed. Women had to feed their husbands
and their families, since the wages paid to their
husbands, fathers, sons, and brothers were very
low. The Ameru slowly became integrated into
the colonial state.

John Mtu Mugambi, the last great shaman of the Meru people, converted to Catholicism in 1974 without passing his legacy of shamanism on to his son. This is evidance of the changing Meru culture.

Traditional councils of elders in each community have been replaced by the central government of Kenya and the State. There are two local major authorities known as Meru Municipal Council and Meru County Council. These councils oversee the political, economic, and social issues of the divisions, replacing the roles of precolonial elders.

Farming has changed, too. While people used to grow a few crops just to feed themselves and their community, farmers must now grow cash crops to survive. There are taxes to pay, so people must have money. Cattle no longer represent wealth in a world where cash is necessary. Education has become more important than bravery to become a respected, successful person.

The individual is a more important element of society now. Land was once owned by a community or by an ethnic group, or by whatever farmer or cattle grazer happened to be using it. During colonialism, land began to be bought and sold. It "belonged" to a certain person who paid money for it. In this way, an individual could gain more power than he or she could ever have had in traditional societies.

In these ways, the Ameru are becoming a part of the global market. The government of independent Kenya is concerned with being considered part of the modern world, not the Third World. Because of this concern, many of the changes brought by the British, such as private ownership of land and the need to grow cash crops, have been further encouraged by the new government.

The biggest trend is still that of cash crops. Tea, coffee, and pyrethrum are crops that the Kenyan government encourages because they earn a lot of money in foreign trade. Livestock, especially that of grade cows for milk, is sold under cooperatives. Beekeeping for honey and wax production are other encouraged activities.

Western education for Meru children has become important in recent years.

Because the population is growing and ever more crops are being grown, new methods to help save the soil from exhaustion are being developed. Soil and water conservation, con-

Beekeeping for honey and wax are encouraged. This man is carrying a beehive made from a tree.

struction of terraces and grass strips, and irrigation schemes for the production of vegetables are all projects that the government is working on to help farmers grow more. Other concerns for the future include conservation of and alternative sources of energy.

In Kenya 75 percent of energy for cooking and heating comes from wood fuel and charcoal. In Meru, 90 percent of the people depend on

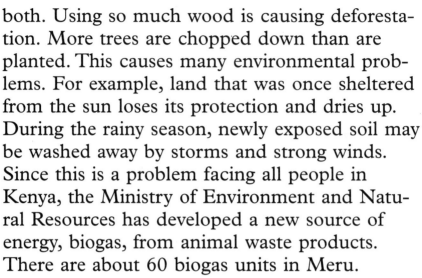

both. Using so much wood is causing deforestation. More trees are chopped down than are planted. This causes many environmental problems. For example, land that was once sheltered from the sun loses its protection and dries up. During the rainy season, newly exposed soil may be washed away by storms and strong winds. Since this is a problem facing all people in Kenya, the Ministry of Environment and Natural Resources has developed a new source of energy, biogas, from animal waste products. There are about 60 biogas units in Meru.

Education and health services are of importance in rural areas. Education in primary, secondary, and technical schools is a concern for the district. There has been an increase in the number of primary schools, as well as an increase in enrollment since 1984. However, there is not enough funding to provide books or other important tools for the schools. Some families are poor, and after paying school fees and buying school uniforms, there is not much left for books, paper, or transportation.▲

chapter

7

CONCLUSION

THERE IS MUCH TO BE DONE BEFORE THE problems of developing, independent Kenya are solved. Policymakers and the government should also be concerned with the consequences of their development programs. Production policies should go hand in hand with the development of health facilities, energy, clean water, infrastructure, education, and enough food. Education in this venture is very important.

There is also a lot to learn, both on the part of the government and the Kenyan ethnic groups. It is important to recognize the shift in gender roles in society. It is equally important to keep in mind the Meru idea that the earth is the great mother and should be respected, especially while farmers produce more and more crops.

The balance of progress and tradition is never easy. The Ameru continue to struggle, along with all the peoples of Africa, to be an active part of the modern world, while also keeping their proud identity.▲

Glossary

agriculture Farming.

biogas Form of fuel made of animal waste products, intended to ease the energy crisis in Kenya.

bridewealth Gift of livestock and honey that must be given by a young man to his bride's parents.

cash crops Crops grown especially to sell, rather than to use.

gichiaro ("birth") Ritual to bind people to each other and to a common ancestor (*ba-gichiaro*: people bound together by this ritual).

kiama Parliament of the elders in Meru society, in charge of law and order.

Mbwaa According to Meru oral tradition, the land where their people originated.

Nguu-Ntune (Red Clothes) The people who captured the Meru in Mbwaa, according to tradition.

Njiru, Ntune, and Njeru "Black, red, and white," the names of the three groups of

Ameru who crossed the Red Sea in their escape from Mbwaa.

oracle Person or thing through which the gods communicate with humans.

pyrethrum Crop of Eastern Africa, sold to make insecticide.

savannah Area of land featuring some open ground for farming and some trees.

shaman Person whose role in society is to heal and to communicate with the spirit world.

taboo Act that is forbidden by a community because it is believed to bring bad luck.

zebu Tough breed of cattle traditionally raised in Kenya because it can survive the difficult climate.

For Further Reading

Bernardi, Bernardo. *The Mugwe, A Blessing Prophet: A Study of a Religious and Public Dignitary of the Meru of Kenya.* Nairobi: G.S. Were Press, 1989.

Fadiman, Jeffrey. *The Moment of Conquest. Meru, Kenya, 1907.* Athens: Ohio University Press, 1979.

——. *An Oral History of Tribal Warfare: The Meru of Mt. Kenya.* Athens: Ohio University Press, 1982.

——. *Oral Traditions of the Meru, Mwinmbe, and Muthambe of Mt. Kenya.* Nairobi: Cultural Division, Inst. for Development Studies, University College, 1970.

Mbise, Ismeal R. *Blood on Our Land.* (Fiction). Dar es Salaam: Tanzania Publishing, 1974.

Moore, Sally Falk. *The Chagga and Meru of Tanzania.* London: International African Institute, 1977.

Ramsay, Jeffress. *Global Studies: Africa,* 5th ed. Guilford: The Dushkin Publishing Group, 1993.

Index

ABOUT THE AUTHOR
Born and raised in Kenya, Esther Wangari received a BA from Warren
Wilson College, and an MA and a PhD from The New School for Social
Research. She has worked as a researcher, an instructor of
microeconomics and international trade, and an evaluation consultant for
the Office of Research of the New York City Board of Education.
    Dr. Wangari has published numerous papers on topics including
women and land reform in Kenya and land tenure in Kenya. She is
coauthor of the forthcoming book *Towards a Feminist Political Ecology:
Global Perspective from Local Experience*. She currently teaches at St.
Cloud University, St. Cloud, Minnesota.

PHOTO CREDITS: CPM, Nairobi
PHOTO RESEARCH: Vera Ahmadzadeh with Jennifer Croft
DESIGN: Kim Sonsky